Jill Biden

Educator & First Lady of the United States

by Elizabeth Andrews

Abdo
HISTORY MAKER
BIOGRAPHIES
Kids

abdobooks.com

Published by Abdo Kids, a division of ABDO, P.O. Box 398166, Minneapolis, Minnesota 55439.
Copyright © 2022 by Abdo Consulting Group, Inc. International copyrights reserved in all countries.
No part of this book may be reproduced in any form without written permission from the publisher.
Abdo Kids Jumbo™ is a trademark and logo of Abdo Kids.

Printed in the United States of America, North Mankato, Minnesota.

052021

092021

THIS BOOK CONTAINS
RECYCLED MATERIALS

Photo Credits: Alamy, AP Images, Getty Images, iStock,
Seth Poppel/Yearbook Library , Shutterstock PREMIER

Production Contributors: Teddy Borth, Jennie Forsberg, Grace Hansen
Design Contributors: Candice Keimig, Pakou Moua

Library of Congress Control Number: 2021932503
Publisher's Cataloging-in-Publication Data

Names: Andrews, Elizabeth, author.

Title: Jill Biden: educator & first lady of the United States / by Elizabeth Andrews

Other title: educator & first lady of the United States

Description: Minneapolis, Minnesota : Abdo Kids, 2022 | Series: History maker biographies | Includes
    online resources and index.

Identifiers: ISBN 9781098208905 (lib. bdg.) | ISBN 9781098209049 (ebook) | ISBN 9781098209117
    (Read-to-Me ebook)

Subjects: LCSH: Biden, Jill--Juvenile literature. | Presidents' spouses--United States--Biography--Juvenile
    literature. | Educators--United States--Biography--Juvenile literature. | First ladies--Biography--Juvenile
    literature.

Classification: DDC 973.099--dc23

Table of Contents

Early Life & Education

Jill Tracy Jacobs was born on June 3, 1951. She grew up with four sisters. The family lived outside of Philadelphia, Pennsylvania.

Pennsylvania

After graduating high school, Jill studied English at the University of Delaware. She continued her education and earned a Doctor of Education in 2007.

The Biden Family

Jill met **Senator** Joe Biden and his two sons in 1975. Two years later, the couple married. They added a daughter to the family in 1981.

THE

From Second Lady to First Lady

In 2009, Joe became vice president of the United States with President Barack Obama. As Second Lady, Jill focused on things that were important to her, like military families and women's health.

Jill also wanted to follow her **passion** for education. She traveled around the US to promote **community colleges**.

In 2019, Joe announced that he was running for president. He won the election in November 2020. Jill became First Lady of the United States on January 20, 2021.

As First Lady, Jill led a program called Joining Forces. It helped take care of military families.

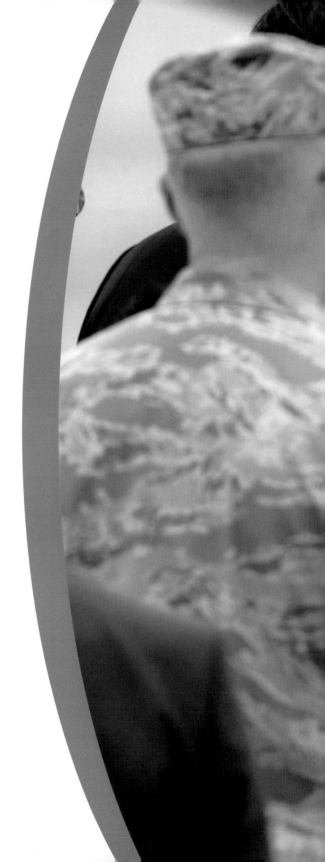

Jill worked hard for teachers and students from inside the White House. It was very important to her that every person gets a good education.

19

Dr. Jill Biden served her country from outside of the White House too. As First Lady, she continued to teach at a Virginia **community college**. She was the only First Lady to work a day job while in the White House.

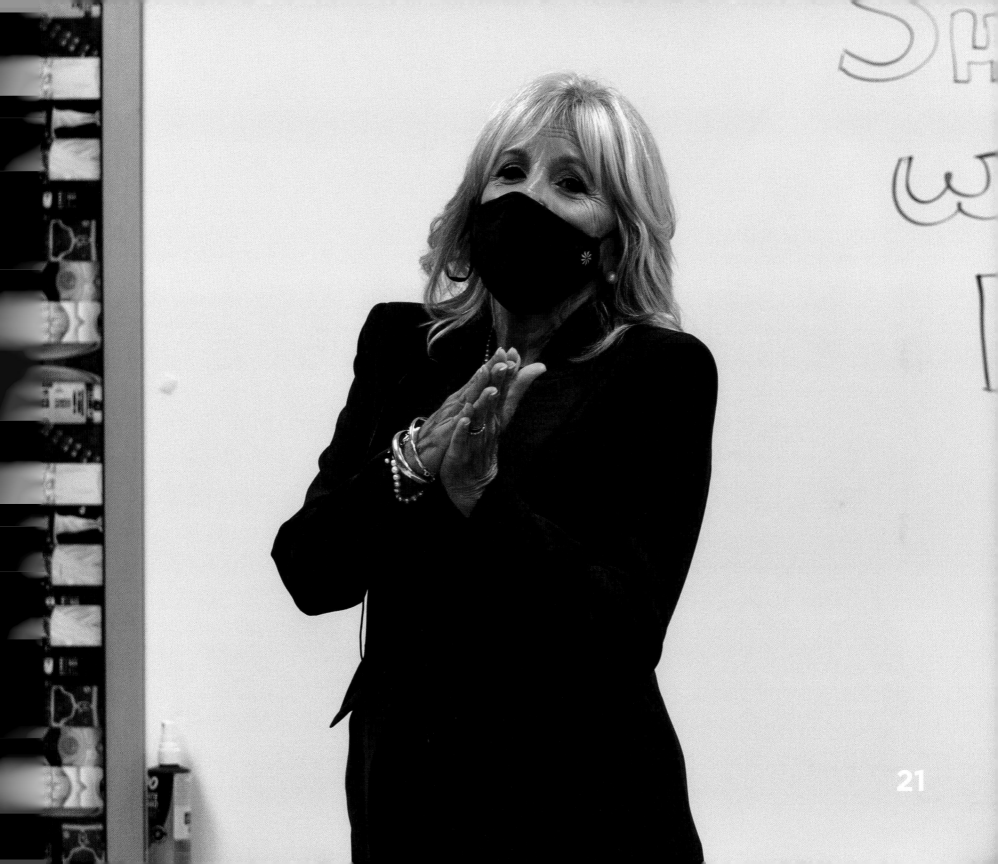

Timeline

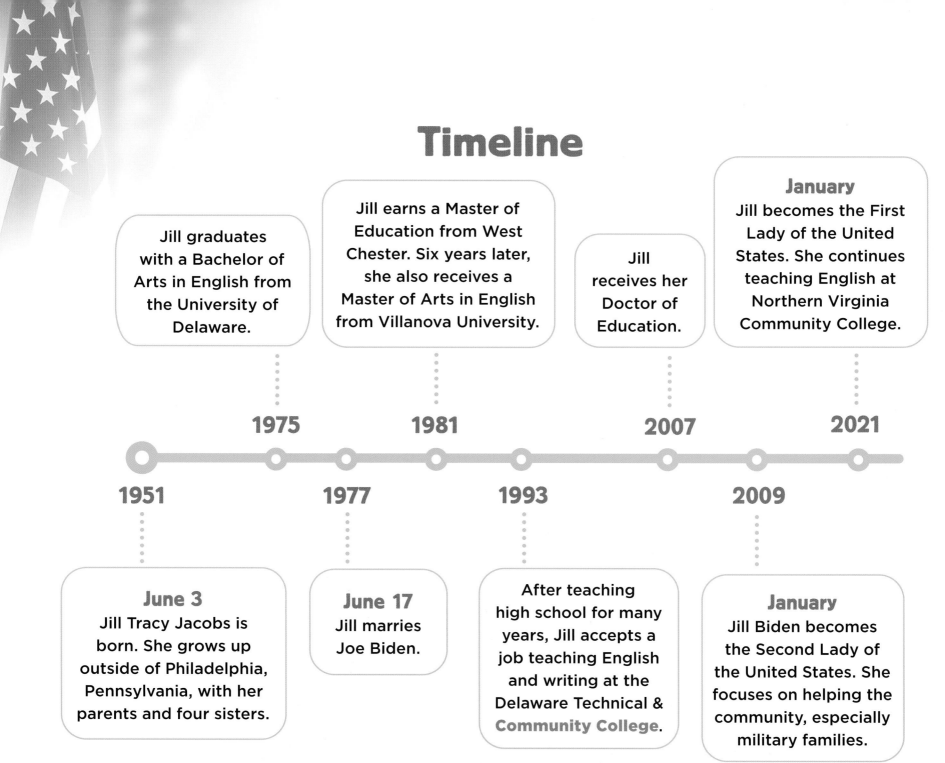

Jill graduates with a Bachelor of Arts in English from the University of Delaware.

Jill earns a Master of Education from West Chester. Six years later, she also receives a Master of Arts in English from Villanova University.

Jill receives her Doctor of Education.

January
Jill becomes the First Lady of the United States. She continues teaching English at Northern Virginia Community College.

1975

1981

2007

2021

1951

1977

1993

2009

June 3
Jill Tracy Jacobs is born. She grows up outside of Philadelphia, Pennsylvania, with her parents and four sisters.

June 17
Jill marries Joe Biden.

After teaching high school for many years, Jill accepts a job teaching English and writing at the Delaware Technical & **Community College**.

January
Jill Biden becomes the Second Lady of the United States. She focuses on helping the community, especially military families.

Glossary

community college – a junior college primarily serving, and often funded, by its local community.

passion – a strong liking for something that one commits time and energy toward.

program – a set of related measures and activities with certain long-term goals.

senator – a member of the Senate. The Senate is one of two houses in the US Congress that has the power to vote on new laws.

23

Index

Abdo Kids
ONLINE
FREE! ONLINE MULTIMEDIA RESOURCES

Visit **abdokids.com** to access crafts, games, videos, and more!

Use Abdo Kids code

HFK8905

or scan this QR code!